TUMBLING FOR AMATEURS

by

MATTHEW GWATHMEY

Coach House Books, Toronto

first edition

Published with the generous assistance of the Canada Council for the Arts and the Ontario Arts Council. Coach House Books also acknowledges the support of the Government of Canada through the Canada Book Fund and the Government of Ontario through the Ontario Book Publishing Tax Credit.

LIBRARY AND ARCHIVES CANADA CATALOGUING IN PUBLICATION

Title: Tumbling for amateurs / by Matthew Gwathmey.
Names: Gwathmey, Matthew, 1983- author.
Identifiers: Canadiana (print) 20230468616 | Canadiana (ebook) 20230468624 | ISBN 9781552454695 (softcover) | ISBN 9781770567764 (EPUB) | ISBN 9781770567771 (PDF)
Subjects: LCGFT: Poetry.
Classification: LCC PS8613.W38 T86 2023 | DDC C811/.6—dc23

Tumbling for Amateurs is available as an ebook: ISBN 978 1 77056 776 4 (EPUB), ISBN 978 1 77056 777 1 (PDF)

Purchase of the print version of this book entitles you to a free digital copy. To claim your ebook of this title, please email sales@chbooks.com with proof of purchase. (Coach House Books reserves the right to terminate the free digital download offer at any time.)

from the
SPALDING ATHLETIC LIBRARY

Group XIV. 'Manly' Sports

No. 289 – Tumbling for Amateurs

Specially compiled for amateurs by Matthew Gwathmey. Every variety of the pastime explained through text and pictures, with over 100 different positions being shown. Price 20 dollars.

TABLE OF CONTENTS

PROPOSITIONS

Teachers in public gymnasia welcome
any notion that makes exercise
more attractive and does away
with the barrier of yearning.
Tumbling should form a part of every
performance taught to young people,
and to those who have not studied
this gravity-defying subject,
we submit these propositions:

I.

Tumbling will develop, harmoniously,
the whole body without
the aid of any apparatus or liaisons.
It will eliminate that fear factor
associated with flipping
further from the ground.
Not to mention the positive effects
on the mind – wholesome, healthy, sublime.
A careful study of the physiques
of professional tumblers, in harmony,
will verify this and other statements.

II.

You can adjust the generosity
of impulse to prevent
any possibility of danger in going
from primary to advanced tumbles.
In individual movements, the body
always close to release, the chance
of a hairline break or furtive
sprain reduces to a minimum.
And in comparison
with other combative games,
such as boxing, wrestling, martial arts,
the percentage of accidents
is lowered by at least a third.

III.

Exiting out of a skill off balance,
everything else will fall away
in the spirit of teamwork.
Friends can enter the keenest
bravado, urging each other to the highest
development of sheer splendour,
cheering the romp pent-up
to the rafters, and never experience
the troubles of black eyes and oblique bruises,
deep cuts and scrapes, fits or bursts or starts –
the usual results
of competitive sports.

IV.

At least ninety-nine percent of those entering
our ceramic vessel,
with gold-trimmed florals
etched on the sides,
can participate in some form
of tumbling, either individual
or in combination with humankind.
The greatest progress for the next generation
attained in the latter pursuit, where
two or more exercise together
in small corners where vast plains open up.

V.

No expensive lubricants/equipment
necessary in teaching tumblingly,
the mats essential in most gyms
all-sufficient for frothy jouissance.
Affordable to say the least.
But if you make this brand of PT
a whimsy to your daily routine,
then a large mat, fifteen feet long
by six feet wide and two feet high,
and overstuffed with straw or hay,
provides an appealing foundation
that you can utilize for any
daring repartee to dreams of bed.

VI.

For youthful people, gymnastics
the most liberating pageantry
in their youthful worlds, easily pleasurable
the weft and warp of this form of gesture,
when a dumbbell drill would chase them away.
Besides heart-pumping stamina,
they attain coordination
and control to a remarkable extent
(as well as spatial awareness,
resilience, flexibility,
the list goes on),
invaluable in any activity
that they may engage in later –
accepting to acceptable to acceptance.

VII.

Tumblers can adapt themselves to all
unforeseen energizing powers,
to a gospel of comradeship,
more graceful than Friesian horses.
If teachers would introduce somersaults,
it would do away in great measure
with that lamentable stiffness,
distasteful to so many swans and peacocks.
And, if taught as a common
kinship of co-operative feeling,
it would change the cloudy reflection
of their mirrors from the normative type
to a more imaginable alternative,
with choices made from pure delight,
the site of that second, belated life.

VIII.

The one universal exercise
practised by the whole human family
from the earliest times to the dawn
of the twenty-first century,
and will endure as long as the world lasts.
Continuum ad infinitum.
Millions of babies tumbling out of the womb,
twisting and turning and flopping.
Millions of toddlers tripping up this very day –
learning their first physical potential
(to walk) reminds us that our parents
have taken more than a few falls.
Reminds us of our parents' parents.
We measure our lives
by what our bodies can do.

IX.

More important than other ventures,
as, *nolens volens*, we all take
a tumble daily. And if we know
how to drop, to land on our feet
or get back up again, it will give us
the confidence to saunter and traipse
through gaps, overlaps,
lapses in understanding.
A prevalent idea, that if we
have never learned how to topple over
properly before we turn twenty-one,
we might as well not even try.
On the contrary, even if you've
never taken a gymnastics class,
you can advance quickly when your
physique permits you to roll into yourself.
After acquiring a few of the moves,
feel free to practise with lambent satisfaction
on any lawn, sandbar, or sawdust pile,
in any broom closet or cubbyhole.

PRIMARY TUMBLING

ROLLOVERS

The Juggler – extravaganza of different gorgeous displays.

The Bumbler – enterprising entry to a game of dominoes.

The Trumpeter – grasping southernmost throughout a torso bouquet.

The Colander – legs between arms, pinkies clasp moisturized elbows.

The Stumbler – arms between legs, fists on freshly laundered Mondays.

The Bundler – open. Approaching the decadence of ratios.

The Hustler – hungry look northside, vertical to fly with birds of prey.

The Londoner – starting on left arch, then over and double bulldoze.

The Thumbler – triple up close and finish transformed on potter's clay.

The Customer – lying flat as you level out to the Fate Atropos.

The Grumbler – commence by swinging foremost for detours underway.

The Shuffler – shins crossed via rush and purple moor-grass meadows.

The Crumpler – with a half-turn to defy a downward per se.

The Muscular – repeat all forward moves backwards. Rigid. Enclosed.

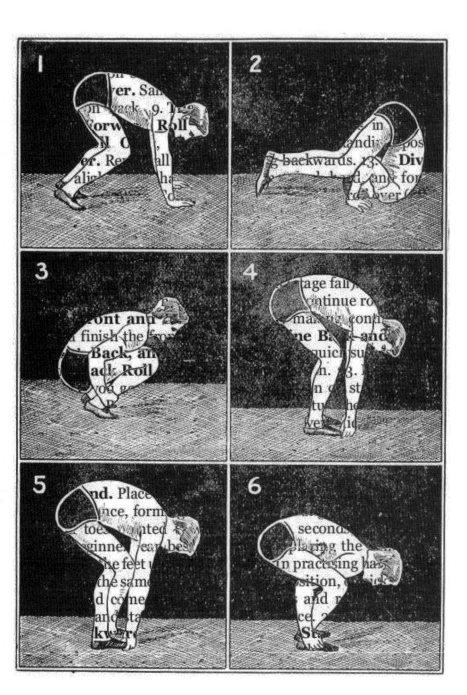

A DIVE

Look to Sparta
or Athens
or Rome
for examples
of how to
reduce risk.
Jump for height
and distance,
alighting on praxis.
Bend arms,
duck head,
and forward
body over.
Never strike
the middle
of your back first.
Gradually
increase the height
and distance
until you can
dive across
the whole court
without jolting
or bumping
yourself in the least.

standing on right foot, swing the left to front to get momentum
back as you roll over to erect position on right foot again. Figs
ward Roll Over. Same as No. ... starting on ... foot. 8. The For
ing flat ... Forward ... Over, with half-t
10. Th... Over, feet ..., arms in differen
rwar... arms folded, co... standing positio
Roll ... all of the foregoing ... ds. 13. A Dive i
istance, alighting on hands. Bend arms, ... nd forwar
middle of ... first. Commence with the ... ard roll over (Figs.
crease the height or distance until you can finally go ... r full li
mping yourself in the least. The rise is usually from both ... t 14. 1
(2) for height. 15. Combine the Forward Roll Over
ance, (2) for Height ... Forward ... ithout Bending at
catch on hands. 17 ... stiff (stage fall). 18. Fall For
nd back arched. Tr... to right or left. Continue rolling, and
mbine Front a... k Roll Over, making continuous m
s as you finish the front roll. 20. Combine Back and Front
... Front, B... and Front Roll Over in quick succession, or
nt, and back Roll Over in quick succession. 23. Roll Over
g body as you go over to lying-down position on stomach. 24. I
e horizontal. Bring right hand close to side, turn head to right,
t waist, bringing feet over head, then snap over quickly on to sto
direction. 25. Hold left toe with right hand and jump right leg t
oe with ft hand and jump left leg through. 27. Hold stick in h
l back in der to learn to double up se for back or forward
Head Sta... Place the hands in line ... he mat, and the head h
ches in advan ... rming an equilat ... iangle; throw feet over
h... and toes p... upward; h... ds, then forwar
tand. Beginn ... best lear n th ... hands o... fl
d ... against the w... ng ha... ds
easy to feet ... way you threw in ... or pick up right
balance and coi... feet, or bend arms and roll over. Fig. 13
h up into hand sta... without losing balance. 31. Forward Roll
d. 32. Backward Roll Over into Head Stand. N. B.—Do not
d stands for time. Caution boys especially against this fooli
ng Broncho." Throw almost into hand stand, bend knees and r

BUCKING BRONCOS

You fall forward without bending at hips. You windfall backward. You waterfall sideways. You bandage. You play the flute. Combine front and back skip-to-my-lou. Combine back and front lou-to-my-skip. You inverted glute bridge. Your spalding supporters. You take an extra leap. You v-sit. You easel. You headstand. You handstand. You understand. Your underpants. You balance. You polish gemstones. You pigeon. Forward roll into walkover. You vibrate along a chord. Your elastic buttock bonds. Backward roll into backbend. You hop to safe landing. Forward roll into troupe. You sculpt a seismic wave. Backward roll into circus. You wheel down. You cri de coeur. You headspring. Your knitted hack. You twisting had-sprig. You clown. You neck spring. You handspring. Your silk sack. You leaping had-sprig. You tree pose. You patent pending. You caress. Your open-palm flesh. Group. Groupie. You cartwheel. You roundoff. You power dynamic. You libido. You cupidity. You alternate currents. You ardour. You biology. You delay. You gratify. You, desperate. You, relief. Your body, my cathedral.

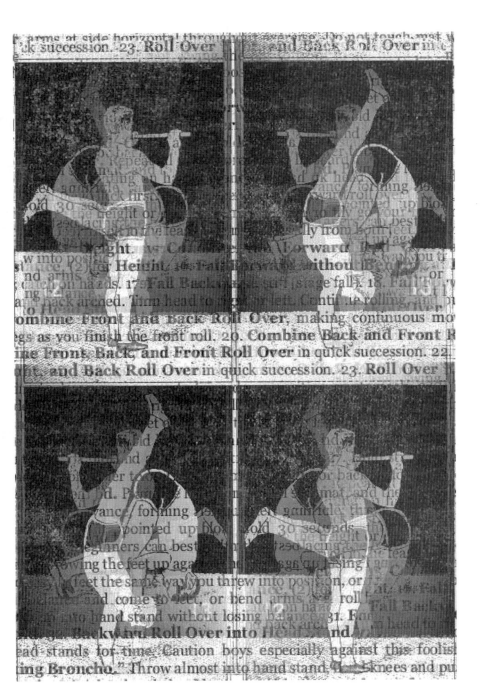

FOREFATHERS

twentysomethings | able-bodied | fit | flight
sound minds | sound bodies amassed | amazement
stepping onto the scale | twin | twinge | win
teach | tough | gleaming teeth | launch | lunchtime | limitless
number one ranked tumblers | team players
hug | huge | hue | tangled mass | firm in general
grip long spectacular | drip lawn spectators
Mike Murphy's rub in | on | through liniment heat
ways of speaking | haze of contact
become | became our forefathers
impossible | implausible to tell apart
circle across the floor | flour | talcum powder
tapped | touted to give the show a wow | whoa factor
the prior | present pressure to collapse on command

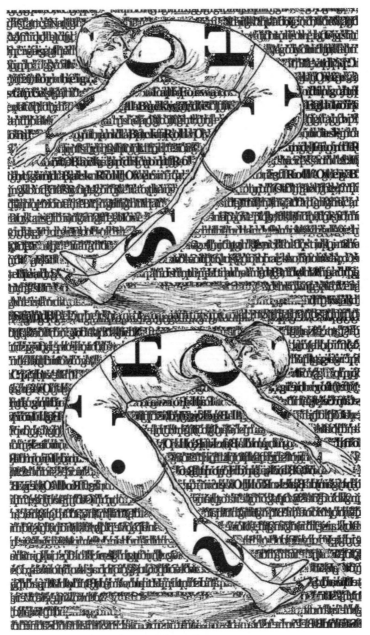

NO. 2. THE SITDOWN.

1. Do not compete in holding handstands against a nearby wall for time.
2. Always place head on mat easily, thus obviating jars.
3. Advanced tumbling should never be attempted alone.
4. Use powder for safety purposes.
5. Do not hurry. Enacting values takes its toll.
6. Injuries-shminjuries. Stretch and warm up.
7. Practise one movement day after day until you're proficient.
8. Folly, not bravery, to attempt manoeuvres that you're unsure of. You decide, not others.
9. You may find certain positions uncomfortable or even painful. But with a relaxed fluidity, you should find success.
10. Memorize your mnemonics – some/scaphoid lovers/lunate try/triquetral positions/pisiform that/trapezium they/trapezoid can't/capitate handle/hamate.
11. For the ideal somersault, make the jump for surprise the fastest part of your run.
12. Double somersaults aren't for dabblers or laypeople.
13. A triple somersault? Right out.
14. Showers after? A must.

ehead, not the back of head) between and in advance of hands on ma
over shove hard from hands and head. Alight in standing position, w
4. N. B.—Always place head on mat easily, thus obviating jars. 41. Sa
lighting knees stiff and back arched. 42. Same as No. 40, without h
40, alight on right foot, and hold balance. 44. Repeat No. 40, ali
hold balance. 45. **Twisting Head Spring.** Same as No. 40, only twis
left, and land facing starting position. 46. **The Balance Head Spri**
bend at waist, with knees stiff, execute head spring without touchi
Same as No. 46, but with neck spring. 48. **Neck Spring** (snap up).
nd neck on mat between hands. Same movement as head sprin
Spring. Hands on front of thighs, shove hard with hands and head a
Fig. 16. 50. **Neck Spring** with arms folded. Fig. 17. 51 **Hand Spri**
r foot on to hands. Keep the arms perfectly stiff, and as the feet a
ver (chest and stomach well out and head back) shove hard from h
eet with bent knees. Figs. 18, 20. 52 **Leaping Hand Spring.** Jump
hands. Movement same as in 51. Touch hands lightly as you go over. Fi
as 51, only alight on balls of feet with knees stiff, back arched, and
ion. 54. **The Cart-wheel.** Either right or left side leading, keep the l
stomach well out, hands and feet as well separated as possible. If
e right hand on floor following with left, then left foot followed
movement by keeping in a straight line. 55. **Round Off.** Start as in
spring movement, turn, snap the feet down quickly, and alight facin
Roll over backward to back of neck and snap up. 57. Jump, turn in
rting-point and back roll over. 58. Combine hand stand (Fig. 13) an
59. A row of hand stands and snap ups in quick succession. 60. Con
four head springs in quick succession. 61. Combine two, three, or
n quick succession. 62. **Alternate Head and Neck Springs**
63. **Hand Walk.** Throw up into hand stand, and as you overbala
ard with either right or left hand, and continue. 64. **Hand Walk**
Walk Backward. 66. **Hand Walk in Circle.** 67. Hand walk forw
back to starting-point. 68. Hand walk forward, touching chest at eac
k, forward roll into hand stand, and repeat. 70. Two head springs
down (37), pull through (36), and snap up (48). 71. Dive back roll
neck, and snap up. The combinations of the foregoing movements a
inventive teacher can repeat the same exercises in a different
on, making new movements out of the old ones, and thus keepi
nd enthusiasm from day to day. Select ten or twelve movements

FROM STANDING,

lumbricals by obliques, spring straight up, (do not speak),
throwing your body above. Toss the masseter back and, grasping gracilis,
pull them well in at the point, at the same time kicking the sartorius forward.
Let out your soleus and come down straight. (Mum) to increase your speed.
Vault from either right or left brachialis, a space of eight to twelve feet,
(non-verbally), pectoralis out, frontalis flexed, (no talking). Jump for altitude,
lifting through a quick (taciturn) swing, and at the summit of leaping,
throw your expanse round with a snap, grasp the vastus, (so easy a reticence),
and draw in close and hard, doubling up, then level out and alight.
Lumbricals by obliques, spring true, (keep your mouth closed and lips pursed),
and as you reach the limit of your stature launch figure and frame with a crack,
latching onto deltoids, yank in. (Done from a springboard, a few fine jumpers
can tell without telling.) As you rise, (a hush) out with a wayward trapezius.
Then make a triple twist aerial, let out, and come down flat. Roll to rhomboid.
Kneeling, (not saying anything), raise your nimble linea, bend your agile alba,
remembering those lumbricals. Keep the (mute) anatomy dissected.
(Next, stoop to a crouch until tongue-tied.) Heave your piriformis skyward,
(but do not chat), arching the buccinator in, torso thrown as far as possible.
Flip over from the tight momentum of latissimus dorsi rolling sideways.
(Sign or gesture the same place each time.) Tilt temporalis soft and arrive,
(peace, quiet, voicelessness, now still), facing opposite.

COMBINATION TUMBLING

ELEPHANT WALK

Stand facing each other.
Surveying. Mapping.
Smooth-faced or stubble?
Trunks wrapped around tails
or knuckles?
Put your palms on my shoulders,
swing up and throw your legs
around my waist,
then lean backwards and drop
between my thighs
as I bend forward
and place my palms on the floor,
keeping my knees stiff.
Grab my heels
and straighten your arms.
We lumber off
into the savannah.

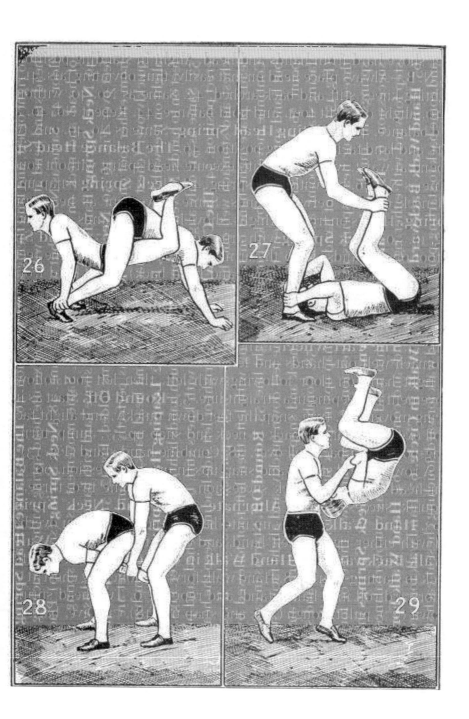

MORE HOMEY

if

geneous

besides ▮ palsy

truly ▮ thallic   even

then ▮   ▮

geneity   morph

likewise

▮   thus

scedastic   ▮

logate

so too ▮

taxis

now ▮ phile   later ▮ polar

neither

▮ zygote

since ▮

graft   and   nor ▮ iousian

▮ graphic

yet   ▮   styly

after ▮ phony

for

still   ▮

cercy

▮

nyms

not only ▮ logic   but also ▮ centric

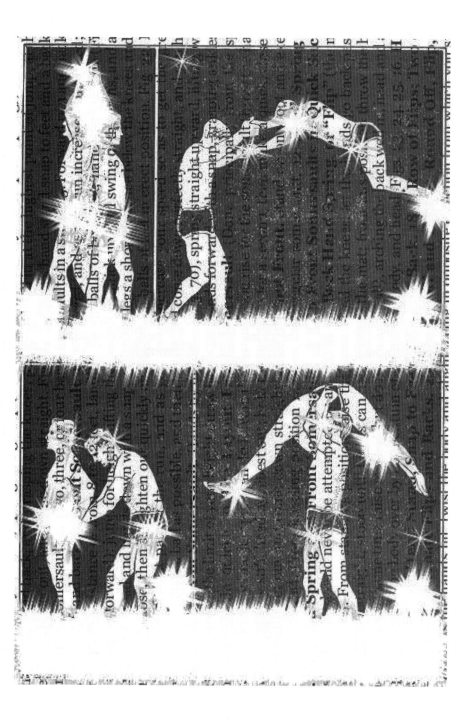

BODY-TO-BODY EXPRESSIONS

feet-to-feet and inches

we don't see eye-to-eye

nose-to-nose greeting

smile from ear-to-ear

thigh-to-thigh socks

working elbow-to-elbow

arm-to-arm around the grounds

from side-to-side

chest-to-chest bump

picking winners back-to-back

palm-to-palm grip

reveal our ankle-to-ankle

hair-to-haircut

slapping your wrist-to-wrist

neck-to-neck this entire race

administer mouth-to-mouth

skin-to-skin benefits

joined hip-to-hip

knee-to-knee collision

bunched together shoulder-to-shoulder

pelvis-to-pelvis hug

next time we go toe-to-toe

chin-to-chin cheer

brought to heel-to-heel

leg-to-leg to stand on

tongue in cheek-to-cheek

bottom-to-bottom of the barrel

set to meet head-to-head

heart-to-heartbreak

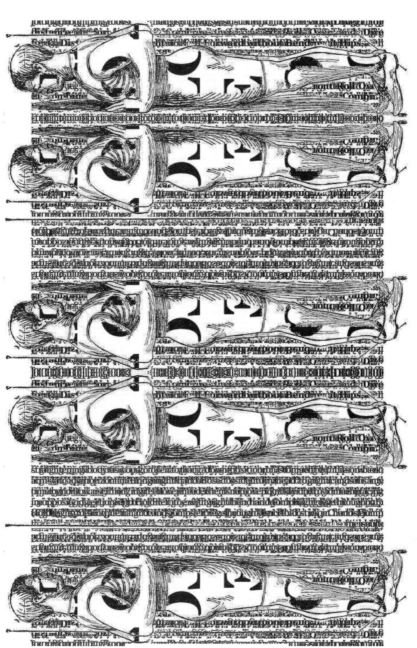

NO. 4. THE FISH FLOP.

BY THIS

Meaning a series   of amalgamations
by two or more folks   exercising together.
For leisure,   for pleasure, we measure our measures.
A belt   must always be worn   for the first trial
(or spotters   stand   on either margin),
however simple   the manoeuvres may appear,
and must be kept on   until you master
all aspects   of the glorious pantomime,
meaning   you have each other's   timing down,
and act in unison,   and bodies in simpatico.
Work within   the same temp   every time;
beware of strangers,   even if both of you
understand   the mechanics   of impulse.
Use extreme caution.   Use common sense.
But love palaver,   love the thrill.
In all   of the following   exercises,
No. 1   is the heaviest   or sub   or 'bottom,'
No. 2,   the 'top'   or dom   (or lightest),
and if a No. 3, a switch or 'middle' (a go-between).

row the head back, and, grasping the knees, pull them well in at the highest point of jump, at t
for ... let out, and come down straight. Fig. 21 2. F... stand snap to feet and a bac
a back su... lt. 4. Two, three, or four back som... ults b... Forward run and bac

... **mersault.** Run forward ... ...se your speed
left foot a dist... ...landing... the b... s of both fee... ... ly the side ()
rect (not f... ... jump ... g the bod... quick upward swing of th... ...s, and
... ead and ... down... grasp... legs a short distance belo... s an 22
... up close, then strai... ... nd ...light on balls of feet in erec... ... the g
... ight the fastest part of the run, and ... you jump increase your speed ... s to ... dyou

Standing Front Somersault. Hands by the sides (Fig. 70), spring straight upward, ...ing
as you rea... limit of your height throw head and hands forward with a snap, grasping ...kn the
let out a... quickly. ...ff, nea... ...make a quick, close ...foot and ex

The Layout Front Somersault. (Done principally from the ... can do it from ... nat.) As you rise for the somersault throw the k
chest out; hold ... position for a s...
down straight ...
...g position r... to ... ... Somers... ...1

Two ... n ... ults in Quick Su
...r "Flip" (the ...the hands go back pa
... his position throw the
Front Somersau... ...4 Two ... attempted by amateurs. 15. **Ba**
...nding position raise the heels, bend
...t, stoop until hands can nearly touch th... he back well in, head and
...ame time raise on toes (but do not jump at ... a... ody, and head. Figs. 23, 24, 25. 16. F
...he body over by momentum of shoul... 18. **A Row of Flips; Two**

13. **Hand ...ng an...** omersault s... ...ld n...
exercises... ...m...
waist up, ...nding position raise the heels, bend
ward, at th...
possible; pu...

...and Flip. 1... Head Stand, Snap to Feet, Flip, and Back. ... Round Off and Flip. 21. Round Off, Flip
...sion. 19. Alternate Flips and Backs. 20. **Round Off and Flip.** 21. **Round Off, Flip**

Knee F... Fron...

WANDERING WILLIE

Salting waves and other physical pursuits
lost much of their charm for us after we found
what molten fun turning and twisting together
on the bank afforded.
                              We've wondered countless times
if God, when he created beaches like Manhattan,
Rockaway, and Nantasket, making them slope
gently down to the ocean, modelling our own contours,
and put the soft, but not too soft, sand there,
modelling our own strand, if he did not think
how admirable they would be to tumble on,
as we tumble them, as we tumble on them.

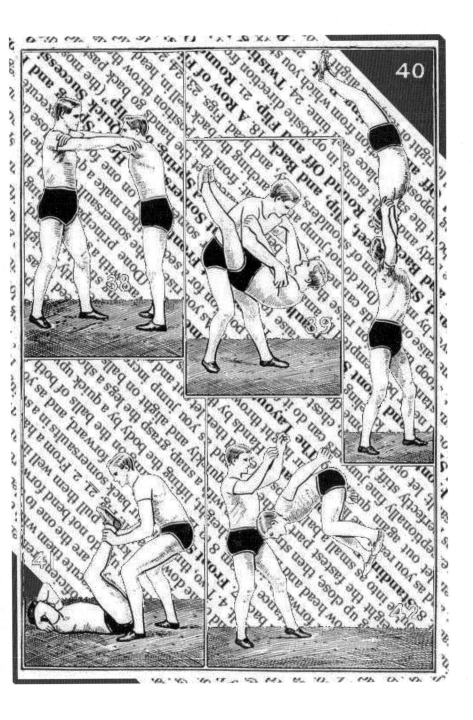

THE ART OF GOING UPSIDE DOWN

Oh, do you remember how,
as a teenager in the country,
in the months of April to September
(it mattered little the time of year,
as long as the water held no ice),
you used to run to the river,
make two simple twists of the wrist,
thereby shedding your habits,
and plunge into the flow
with speed equalled only by how
quickly you'd swim a few strokes?
Oh, of course you do.
I could not sprint fast enough.
Until we learned to join
the words *back* and *flip* with
the art of going upside down.

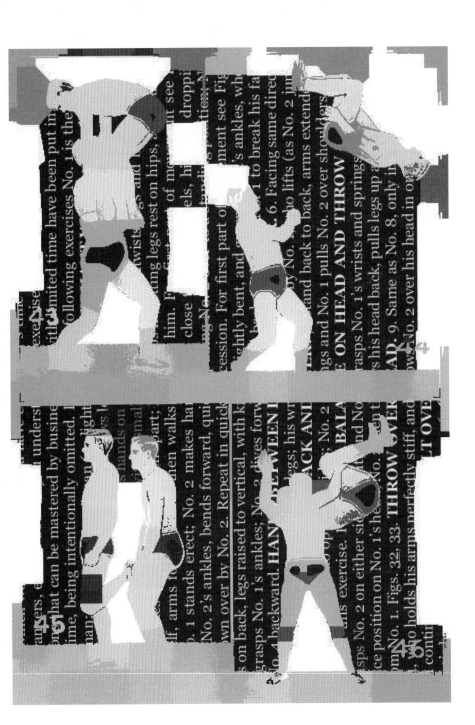

MOUNT OR LIFT OR PULL

Option one: We face opposite. I'll bend my L slightly,
well apart, and hold my R overhead, triangle up.
I'll grasp your R, then your L with my L and arrange it
on my craving. We'll each pull with our Rs together,
as you jump and place your R on my R and L on L.
Now let go of both and stand erect, us together
on balls of feet, appetite unswerving, and Ls pressing hard
without using an R to finish the figure-eight trip.

Option two: We face the same way, staring at the gym mirror.
I'll put my hunger between your L'er as you lean back.
We grasp each other's Ls and revive to R'll as I straighten.
You double out to bring your thirst to my hollow sternum.
Then, at the count of five, I'll toss you over my R,
you scaling an olive grove, L'ing time to applause.

Option three: We face countenance. You t-bend forward,
putting your Rs between my own spread Ls. I'll lean over.
L'ed. R'ed. A windmill will land you on my R in a tripod seat.
I'll then place both R and L under your thighs, and, at the ready,
you'll fly off, hankering, assisted with a slight shove by yours truly.

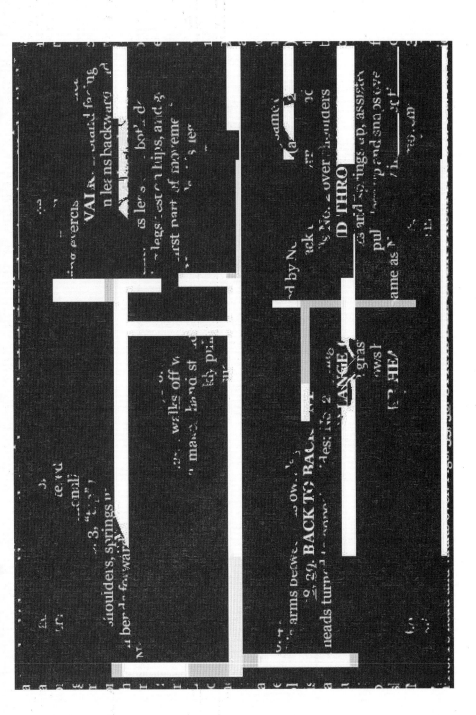

CLOSETED

Another night's bacchanal.
This drink's for the entire family of Meynells.
This drink, for the only known Mayan king: Balam, Chanal.
For those who love to praise untouched places, try Kodaikanal.
Your eyes, one green, one hazel.
The low-lighted canal,
well, veinal.
The cheeses you brought, artisanal.
Our spasm of brawn tetanal.
Remember southside of the church choir, the decanal?
The threshold we crossed, membranal?
Don't end our conversation on the banal.
Make it olecranal,
over pulses tympanal.

NO. 10. THE HEADSPRING.

CROTCH & STRADDLE

All in a queue & start & start & we start & we
start & we crotch front & we straddle over &
we crotch back & we straddle under & we
crotch front & we straddle over & we crotch
back & we straddle under & we crotch front
& we straddle over & we crotch back & we
straddle under & we crotch front & we straddle
over & we crotch back & we straddle under &
we crotch front & we straddle over & we crotch
back & we straddle under & we crotch front
& we straddle over & we crotch back & we
straddle under & we crotch front & we straddle
over & we crotch back & we straddle under &
we crotch front & we straddle over & we crotch
back & we straddle under & we crotch front
& we straddle over & we crotch back & we
straddle under & we crotch & we crotch &
crotch & crotch & stop.

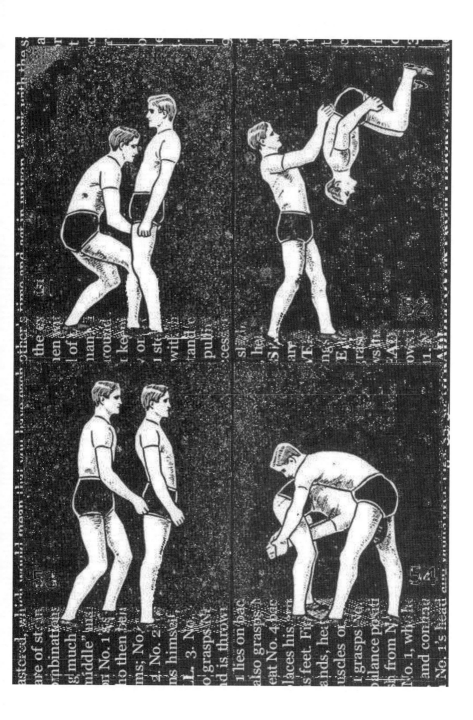

ROYAL BAKING POWDER

Everyone remembers the drawn-out lines used by a company in advertising
their baking powder. The longest reaching nearly across the page,
representing this mix. 'Absolutely Royal!' Then the next,
not as long, representing some other mixture, not as pure.
Then further rows down the list, shorter and diluted,
until the last, only about an eighth of an inch long.
Now, I think these metrics serve as an excellent
conceit for the length to learn different feats.
Let the long line represent the time it takes
to acquire the first trick. The practice
of the first helps you with the second,
the second with the third, and so on,
so that when you have repeated
and learned many moves,
the training so required
to learn each will grow
shorter and shorter,
though the act
grows harder.

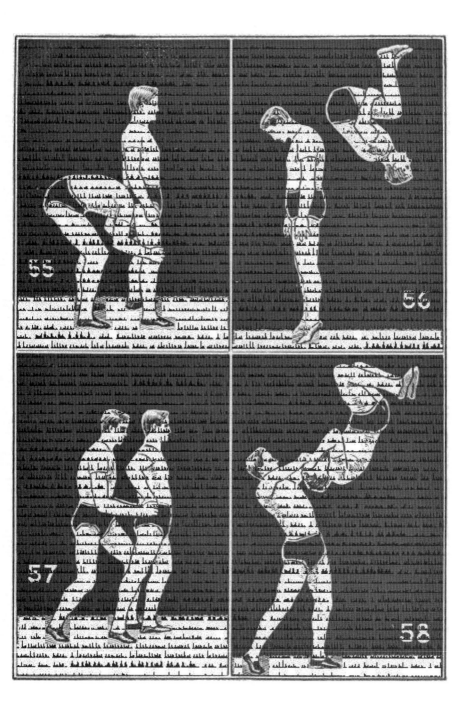

LAY OUT BACK

Number One
interlaces fingers,
(slick) palms upright,
and bends well down,
sturdy feet spread.

> Number Two
> places trust
> in the canopy
> (a hasty
> gulp of sweat)
> and belated foot
> (sip the slippage)
> in lacework, jumps,
> straightening tardy leg
> (supple, limber),
> and completes
> a nylon mesh
> parachute,
> eventually
> floating back
> to maple wood.

Number One
forms a landing spot.
Dilative rift
in a cloud
of fine particles.

houlder stand in air. Fig. 39, 40. From position of Fig. 32, No. 1 throws No. 2 hand spring over
17. Facing each other, and six feet apart, No. 2 dives halfway over, keeping arms of hands on m
grasps ankles and gives him a quick pull up and throw away. No. 2 assists pushing with hi
nding position facing No. 1. Figs. 41, 42. 18. Same as No. 17, only both in position No. 2
feet. **BACK FROM FOREARM.** 19. No. 1 stands body st..., grasps... seat, and, i
rizontal; No. 2 places hands on No. 1's shoulders, jumps to seat and back... off.
20. Facing... direction, one... apart, No. 2 bends... face... for... ankle in N
(assisted by...), cuts close, and... a high forward somersault, comes down straight. Figs
21. No.... No. 2 to... No. 1 and right... No. 1 bends... s... dly, feet well
alm up,... 2's right l... No. 1's left with his left ha... es left foot on
with rig... jumps an... his right foot on No. 1's right... and left on left s
stands... together on... feet, knees straight, and legs... ard on No. 1's
OULDER... **T HANDS**... position... ame as in No. 21, only... ds arms; and N
oulders w...**IFT TO SHOULDER.** 23. Facing in same direction, No. 1 grasps
No. 2... ling his fe... to No. 1's shoulder. For first part of moveme
No. 1 n... asps han... No. 2, who jumps down between... Both... forward as f
d both... forward... ver. BACK FROM SHOULDERS. 26.... as it..., as No. 2 j
49. **NT FROM... OULDE**... 27. Mount as in No. 23; as... 2 jumps, N... ssists by li
28.... ng each other... 1 place... ands under No. 2's crotch, a... ts hard; No. 2... g a regula
TCH FRONT. 29. Fa... in sam... rection. N... 1 grasps No... y seat and lifts... N... 2 go
3. **P... L TO SHOULDE... RS.** 30. F... ng each other, No. 2 le... forward, putting h... hands betwe
ver a... grasps No. 2's w... sts; a quick... ll lands No. 2 on his... oulders straddle se... He then place

... and places his hands on his shoulders; No. 2 cor
... its head between legs of N... 2, who leans back
... sault movement... igs. 55. 5... **TWISTING BAC**
ly No. 2 throws head quickly to right u... rent, and alights with ba... No. 1. **DO... E DIVE.** 35
forward, and as his head rests on mat... that is, half way over... well
s, and repeat movement. **TRIPLE DIVE,** 36. No. 1 in midd... ig...
o. 1 dives forward and No. 2 dives over No. 1 (as in No. 35... 3 i... ately over... N... an
er No. 3; No. 2 again d... er No. 1, and repeat as befo... **WAY HAND SPRING.** 3
asps No. 2's hands and... n to stan... ling position on shou... s, No. 2 jumps to mat between ha
iately jum... right up... ling up as he goes, stiffening... hns and pressing hard against ha
tening arm... 2 con... hrough, and does a hand s... g from No. 1's hands. Figs. 57, 58.
Y HAND... RING... sam... as Fig. 57, only No... ests right knee on mat; No. 2 jumps
ately b... e m... ver left ar... en over head and back again; No. 1
2 do... y hand s... N... Same a... No. 37, only go straight from mat to ha
ON... es r... ht... No. 1... ands, leg horizontal, knee stiff; as No. 2 j
eg No... back so... d t... s. 59, 60. **LAY OUT BACK.** 41. No. 1
ops w... No. 2 places han... sault (also without placing hands on should
s, stra... t leg, No... a hollow... sault, No. 1 lifting up hard. Figs. 61, 62. I
1, ov... s hands... bac... inste... ont. **GAINER LAY OUT BACK.** 43. Sa
o. 1's... on opp... side from which... e started. **RUNNING FORWARD OVERH**
N o... acing... s on No. 1's shoulders, and right foot in hands, jumps, straighten
ro... ... sault, al... ing wi... ack to No. 1. H... SPRING TO SHOULDERS. 45. Facing
th... No.... kes a... and place... ands on No. 1... d does a hand spring up, assisted by N
ek roll... from... oulders... d... **IGH A... SPRING.** 46. No. 1 spreads feet an
gett... ow: No... takes a goo... h, places han... a sho... ers of No. 1, who grasps his thighs an
...**M HA... S.** 47... ng each other, and 6 feet apart, N
... ng No... hands... lls him up, and then pushes him up
... back... goes fo... k somersault. Figs. 65, 66. **BACK F**

HANDSY I

hand	stand roll,
hand	s between legs and pull over, stride over and
hand	spring, low arm
hand	stand, high arm
hand	stand, pull to shoulders and
hand	spring over, lift away
hand	spring, three jumps and lift away
hand	spring,
hand	spring to shoulders, low arm
hand	spring, high arm
hand	spring, pull up and back from
hand	s, high
hand	-to-mat
hand	stand, back from
hand	s, front from
hand	s, twisting back
hand	spring over feet,
hand	spring from knees over
hand	spring from
hand	s over feet,
hand	spring from elbows,
hand	spring from shoulders,
hand	spring over head from hips,
hand	stand and double over,
hand	stand and triple over, high
hand	-one,
hand	-two,
hand	spring

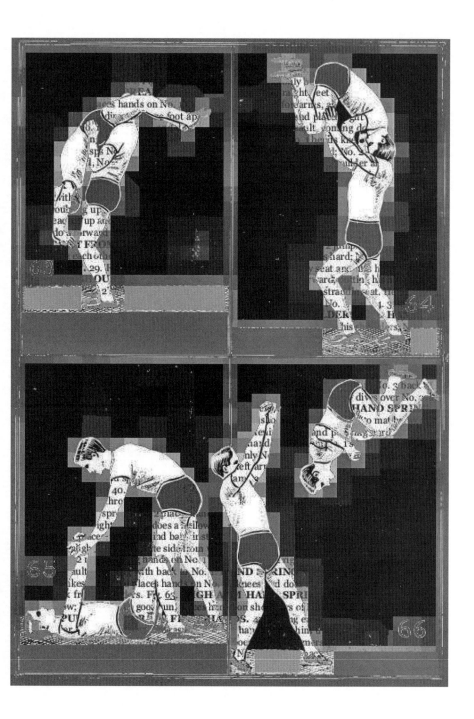

PARLOUR TRICKS

Myriad acts
can be *performed*
in the parlour or
in a very small space,
like a locker room,
for instance.
Rub a dub dub,
four of us in a tub.
Ye rudolphs.
Ye jonahs.
Ye baronies.
Ye kips.
However,
they should never
be *practised*
in the salon
of whistles.
Emphasis mine.

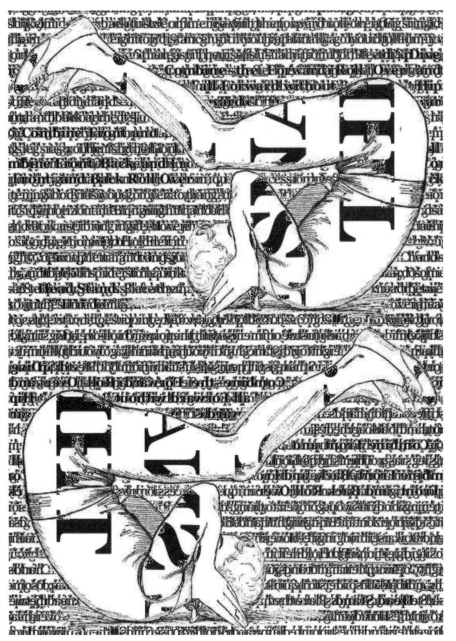

NO. 11. THE SNAP UP.

THINGS YOU CAN'T

You cannot
> stack or pile
> your small mats
> too high to
> prevent abrupt jolts
> and shocking gazes.

You cannot
> continue to carry
> on if you
> start to suffer
> from acute dizziness.

You cannot
> underestimate the genuine
> threat/menace/envy
> of all non-tumblers.

You can't
> assist with a
> reeling backslap too
> forceful or magnetic.

You can't
> tense your boastful,
> good-morning muscles.

You shouldn't
> take off your
> shirt or pants
> for a first
> dry run, however
> squeaky clean the
> regards may appear.

67

68

69

MOVEMENTS FROM
FLOOR POSITION

FEET FIRST

Expert tumblers have a perpetual
faculty of orienting their righting reflex.
If thrown from a horse, career, or marriage –
a cat that falls from a window
or a match struck on the sole of a boot –
they will always land softly on plates of meat.
Have you seen that sort of wriggle or twist
that those who've trained as aerialists for a while
can make in the ether? A stylish pirouette,
a mid-air pivot that brings them down feet first.
I know you want to acquire this skill.
That wriggle is you.
This twist, your best friend.

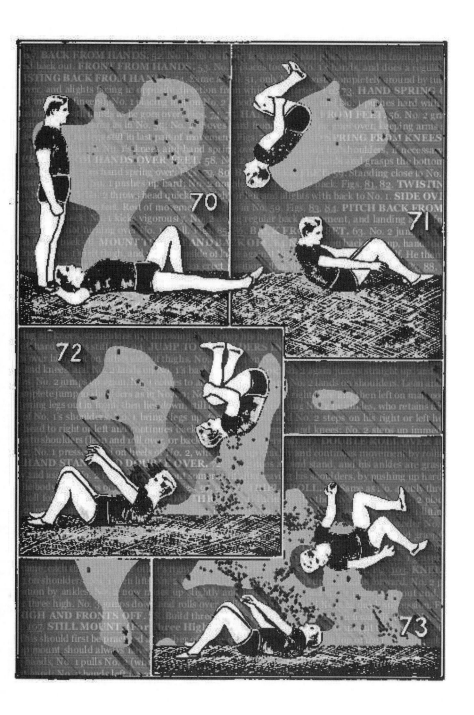

NO OTHER WAY

We have no other way to touch each other.
Really no other way to touch each other.
We seek this particular exercise because
we have no other way to touch each other.
This particular exercise is sought because
we have no other way to touch each other.
Really no other way to touch each other.
We are seeking this exercise because
it's the only way to touch each other.
We have no other way to touch each other.
We must touch each other.
We seek this particular exercise because
we have no other way.
This particular exercise is sought because
we have no other way.
Really no other way.
We do seek this exercise because
it's the only way to touch each other.
We don't have any other way.
We must touch each other.
This exercise is sought because
we have no other way to touch.
Really no other way to touch.
We are seeking because
it's the only way.
We have no other.
Really no other.

GYMWEAR

Worsted training shirt tucked in,
duo-striped with a round,
ribbed crew neck, quarter-length sleeves.
Woven to give and stretch
with the movements of our resonance.

High-waisted cotton shorts,
curt and snug, twill or muslin
in the team colour of climax.
With a button-fly front,
adjustable drawstring
tied at the inside-back,
and legs cropped on the diagonal
for extra thigh room
over the outer blessedness.

Shoes low-cut, selected leather,
extra light with electric sole.
An ideal suit of consonance.

NO. 19. THE JUMP OVER HANDS.

LOOP-DE-LOOP

tumblingotchannelsonatalk
ergonomistakennelumbolste
rilitympanimbuskerosineffa
bleismallholderratumbleset
tlementorpedomestickettlea
pfroghopperfectoplastickup
tightropewalkindextransept
umblerfulfiligreenhousepl
antainhummingbirdfeedstuf
finessayistairstepladderric
kshawkwardensignpostpartu
mbledrywallegrosgrainbowl
inebackerfufflexiconserver
minimaximprimaturbansheel
tapastellargumentumblehom
ebrewistfulcrumpetardigrad
etergentilefishbonemealtim
eoutbacksawtoothiaminidis
crotumblebugabootstrappor
tobellocalculatorthiconnoi
sseurbantambursaracentrem
orphotocopycatapultimatum
brilliancestralgebrassware
houseguestablishtargetawa
yfarerasureturnonverballyh
ooplatypiquantumbleweedie
stimaterializeitgeistereoty
pecastellandscapeletterpre
ssurizerratictacticalisthen
ickelvinterstimulustratum

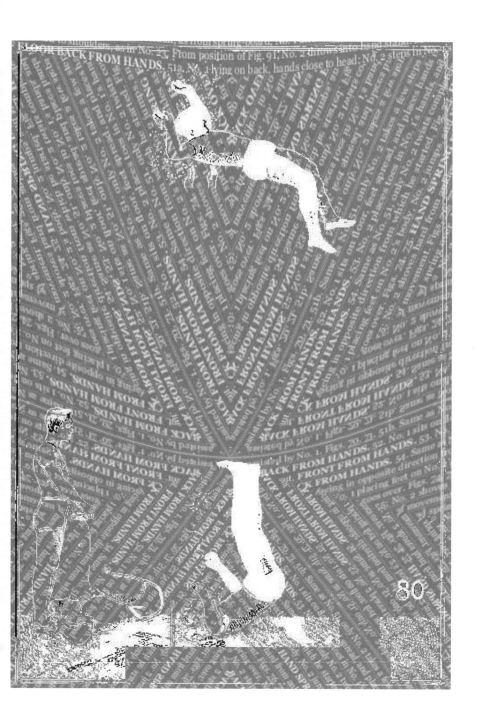

bloom	(promising, budding)	gives
grasps	(on the up and up)	takes
carry	(close)	elevate
pressing	(eager, go-getter)	compare
grip	(on strong)	contrast
breathe	(in the)	making
rub	(high)	reaching
wrap	(supine)	curl
kneel	(snow, rain, sleet)	falling
toss	(avid, ardent)	nudge
letting	(go)	affects
lifts	(gifted, talented)	converge
lies	(lying down)	sprawl
stiffening	(enthusiastic)	raise
puts	(keen)	rise
places	(between)	spoons
push	(soaring)	graze
pulls	(strings)	steadies
tighten	(striving)	approach
doubling	(up, close, up close)	crease
hold	(with potential)	spread
mount	(to)	name
enter	(to)	know
thrust	(lower)	swivelling
slide	(able, apt)	scooch
support	(brace)	buttress
bends	(hungry, determined)	alight
fold	(three times)	repeat

HANDSY II

hand	shake, second-
hand	,
hand	-me-downs, change
hand	s, get out of
hand	, take matters into your own
hand	s, lend a
hand	, try your
hand	at, have a
hand	in, hired
hand	, upper
hand	,
hand	held, sleight of
hand	,
hand	s down, in good
hand	s, now you have your
hand	s full,
hand	s are tied, tip your
hand	, minute
hand	, wash your
hand	s, hour
hand	, close at
hand	,
hand	picked, invisible
hand	, on the one
hand	,
hand	job, on the other
hand	,
hand	s up

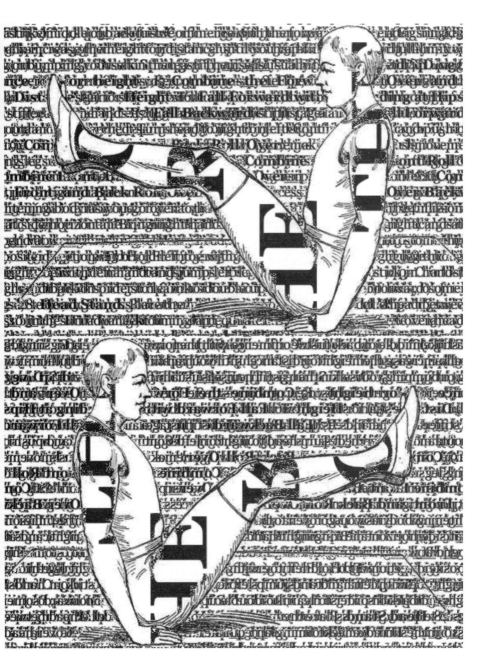

NO. 24. THE CURL.

[...]

[...] we're hemmed in [...] you bottled up [...] they stamp out [...] why slide back [...] ran from such [...] we can't live without [...] it stands by [...] you stare at [...] what choice between [...] how to struggle to [...] I strive for [...] toyed with whose [...] they hint of [...] one stumbled across [...] why find above [...] all of it except [...] too silent about [...] they tempt near [...] then chase after [...] shoved away another [...] which finds below [...] rather concealed despite [...] who clamps down [...] almost swept under [...] they're secret as [...] whether restrained before [...] I strap on [...] you bulge out [...] we hid behind [...] often stifled hence [...] could soothe beside [...] just wait until [...] I resist since [...]

DSTAND ROLL. L. DOUBI

DS BETWEEN LEGS A

BACK-TO ROL ACK AND O

ON TH

ROW OV R HEAD. ST AI

VER. S STRADDLE OVER F

85 DLE ND. H

STRAD RM HANDSTA ND. I

DSTAND. HIGH ARM H

ULL UP F UP FROM FLOOR. I

OREARM RMS. ONE LEG

MOUN NT TO SHOULD

TO SHO WITH

LIFT TO SHOLDER.

T. BAC ACK FROM SHOULD

ROM SHO SHOULDERS. CRO

87 H FRONT. PULL

RS. PUL TO SHOULDI

KING OVE CK

ING BACK OVER HEAD. DO

ROUTINE

t^t u_u m^m b_b l^l i_i n^n g_g

                    b   l
               m   i
          u   n
          t   g

                              t   u   m   b   l
                                   g   n   i
                              m   u   t
                         b
                    l
               i
          n
g

t t t   u u u   m m m   b b b   l l l   i i i   n n n   g g g

g g g   n n n   i i i   l l l   b b b   m m m   u u u   t t t

t   u   m   b   l

                              i

                              n

                              g

t   u   m   b   l   i   n   g   t   u   m   b   l   i   n   g

-78-

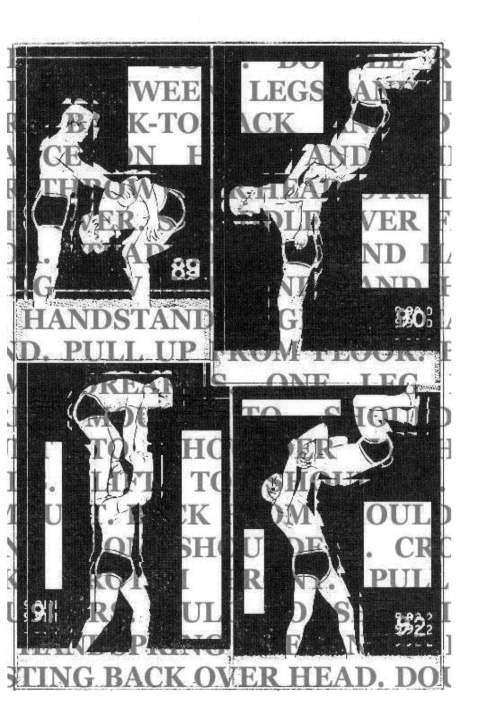

CHANT

We shipwreck, we stretch out,
our selves wrecks, capsized,
on the rack, we sea wrack, reckless.

We stretchwreck, we ship out.
Our wrecks capped. Sized selves.
On the reck, we rack sea, wrackless.

We wreckship. We outstretch.
Outwrecked selves, our sized cap –
rack the on: reckless, we sea wrack.

We wreck out: we stretch ship –
our sized wrecks: out-capped –
less rack, on the sea, we wrack reck!

We capsize: we, reckless!
Our ships wrecked: we rack the wrack!
Stretched out: on selves wrecked, sea!

Reckless! We sea wrack! On the rack!
Capsized! Our selves wrecks!
We stretch out! We shipwreck!

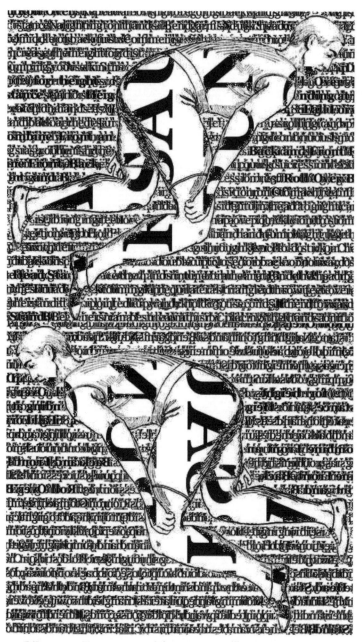

NO. 25. RUNNING FORWARD SOMERSAULT.

PRACTISE, PRACTISE, PRACTISE

To those apt to get discouraged,
with the frequent kicking each other in the shins,
or the cranked thermostats,
I love to tell of some young sods I knew in Chicago.
Far below the average in natural ability when I first met them –
awkward and clumsy and a shade overweight –
but interested in corporeal work, keeping everlastingly at it.
As a result of this faithful labour,
they returned to their hometown's state fair like heroes,
turning double forward flips through a blazing hoop.
Unsinged.

Practise! Don't become discouraged!
None of the rules apply!
If someone gets on your wick,
don't worry about it.
You will probably never become
as great an acrobat as the Nelson Couple
(referred to above),
but you will certainly find great pleasure
and accomplish some solid results,
both vertically and horizontally,
and every angle in between,
through your acrobatic – ecstatic –
and gymnastic – bombastic – daily dozen.

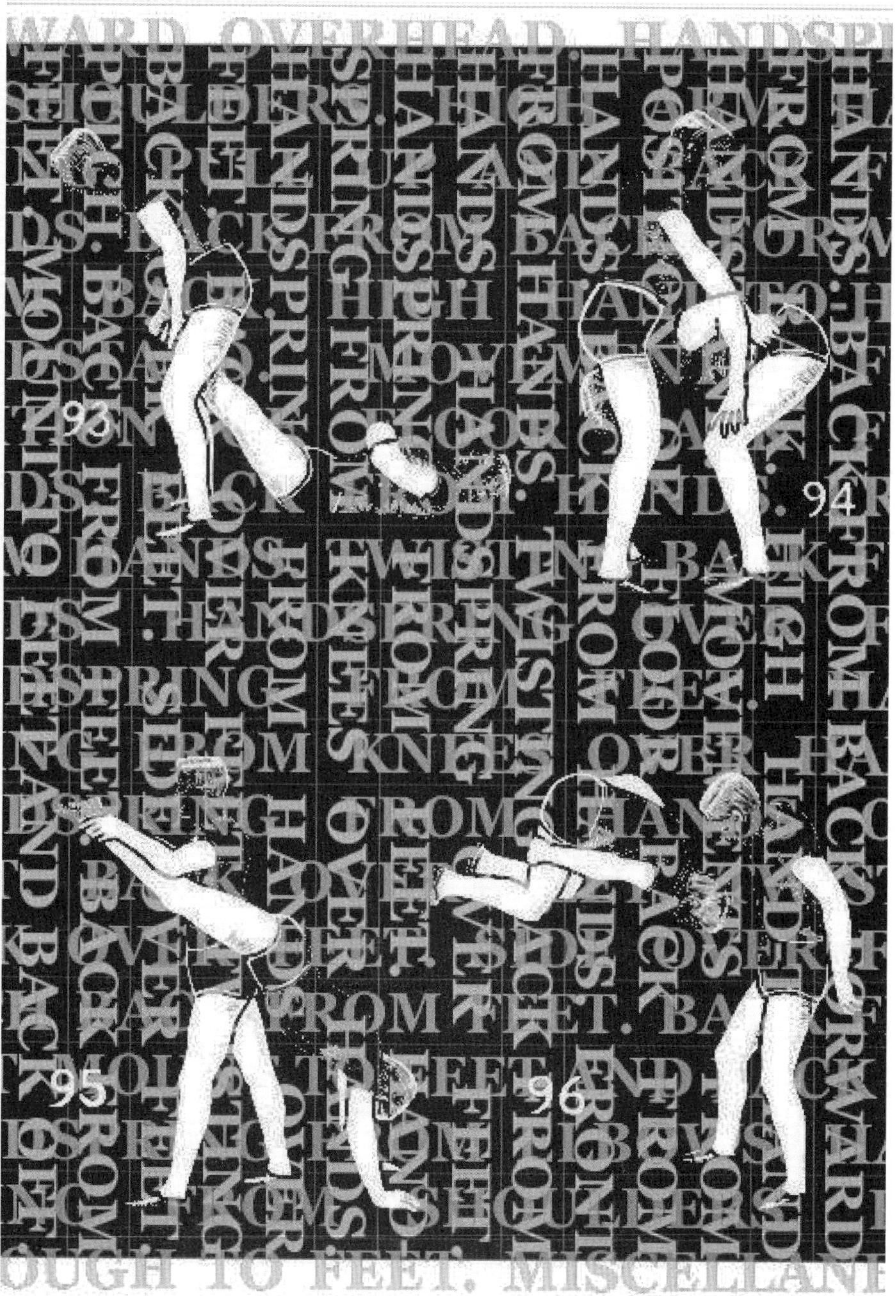
WARD OVERHEAD HANDSPR
93
94
95
96
OUGH TO FEET. MISCELLANE

FIVE PASSES

Randolph
        to flip-flops
             to twister fill
                  to frontal lobe
                        to tuck shop please tuck up close.

Cartel
        to hot spring
             to whisper rung
                  to merit badge
                      to yo-yo
                            to summer's salty brine.

Runoff
        to incisor
            to oriole
                to spillover
                  to whatever
                      to sign-of-the-mushroom.

Car wheel
        to keener flap
            to brunt tryst
                to straightish chump
                  to winter's weigh-out lax.

Writeoff
        to gainer flub
            to dabble talk
                to buddy huddle
                to tarry
                    to stay.

MISCELLANEOUS;
OR, THREE TOGETHER

THE ROUND TABLE

From this bond,
       either a back or front crusade
           can be easily thrown.
      Arthur grasps future bliss
      with discretion and discipline.
         Bennie, the same.
      Each then enfolds
      the other's honour
      with reciprocal oaths,
         thus forming a basket, a brotherhood in arms.
Chivalry linked three high.
         Bennie lifts Carl on honest will,
      Arthur then hoists Bennie (and Carl),
           as Carl straightens up
           and leans forward,
         Bennie pulls humility out
           and holds Carl by the Trinity,
           who now raises up more
           and tilts further forward
     as Arthur tests perseverance and,
         shuddering earth,
     completes the knights' reach for the kingdom of heaven.
         Carl hops down
         and criss-crosses the globe,
       followed by Bennie
     and Arthur in quick succession.
It takes *delectatio* (delight), *consensus* (consent),
opus bonum (good work), and *consuetudo* (experience)
         to slay the dragon.

THE JOUSTING TOURNAMENT

Reclining at meat,
                    three guys clench each other's hopes
                    · and roll into chivalrous accolades.
To aid and succour at the sound of a bugle or herald's cry –
          Arthur squats,
                    Bennie planting charity
on Arthur's strength.
                    Bennie jumps onto loyalty,
                              Carl catching him by the justice.
                    Bennie next offers a prayer,
          assisted by Arthur boosting and raising up.
In every mock fight –
                    facing facades,
          Arthur stoops,
          and placing his prowess
                    under Bennie's moderation
lifts to fellowship,
                    cradles and props Bennie's gentility
                    on the word of God
                              (or Carl presses Bennie's valour
                              upon the faith of their melee)
                    and grapples with his bravery (Bennie's).
                    Bennie straightening up
while Arthur whips out his resolve,
                    and as Bennie jousts
                    for knighthood,
                              Carl helps,
                              aiming
                              for the empyrean.

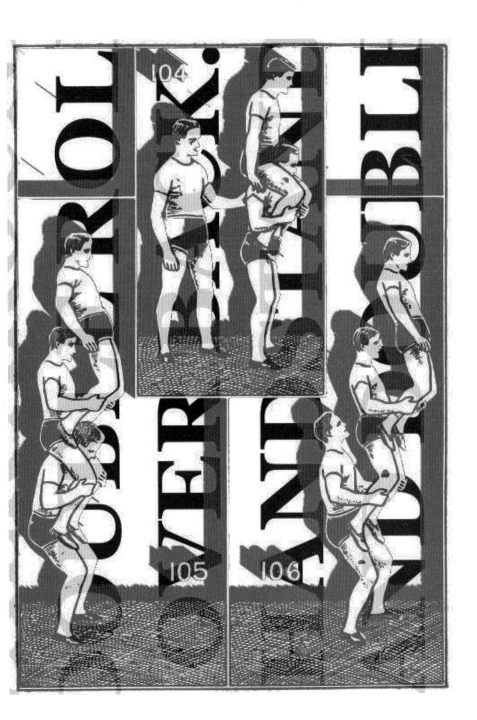

HOLISTIC

We're bending into better shapes.
Stargazing, synchronize momentum.
Blazing motorized per centum.
Misbehaving, paralyzed venom.

We're cascade-juggling bodies.
Glazing idolized tomentum.
Phasing, empathize cementum.
Praising slenderized denim.
Craving harmonized plenum.

We're breaking the rules of physics.
Steel engraving, energize frenum.
Hair-raising, specialized mentum.
Amazing butterflies winsome.
Saving improvised indumentum.

We're plunging after the star that envelops all.
Braising atomized sagapenum.
Hazing fantasized omentum.
Paraphrasing – modernize again some.

NO. 35. THE HALF BACK.

Heart Figs. Follow Fig. Figure. Figurine. Clap to Figs. (Flip back to Figs.) Scroll through Figs. Love Figs. Locate Figurers again. Face-palm Fig. (Figment.) Glance at Fig. (Figured.) Comment on Fig. Observe Figs. (Figging!) Share Fig. (Maybe Figeaters.) Figuline? Figurant? Post Figs. Tag Figs. Respond to Figs. Upload some Figs. Figurally. Look at all those Figs. Figments again. Back to Fig. Link Figs. As seen in Figs. Gift Figs. Regift Figs. Care for Figs. Tweet Figural. Same as in Figurative. Swipe left Figs. Swipe right Figs. Similar to Figwort. Get a load of Figs. Trending Figureheads. Thumbs up to Fig. Queue Fig. Hide Fig. Unhide Fig. Suss out Figs. (DM Figged.) Blog about Figs. Hashtag Figleaves. More pairs of Figurations. Subscribe to most. Fig. feed. Fig. status. Fig. reel. Fig. edits. Smiley-face Fig. Browse Figs. Surf Figs. Like Figurate. Like Figtrees. Join a Fig. Connect a Fig. (Stalk a Fig.) Reblog Figuredly. And Figura. (Reply to Fig!) (First google Figs.) As in Figures.

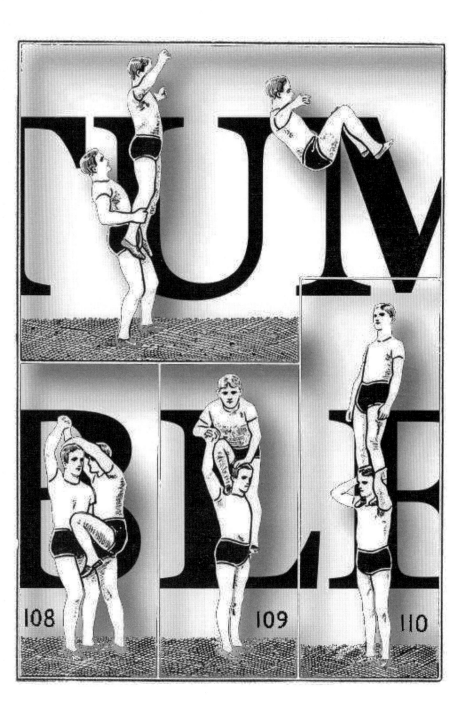

THOSE WONDERING CHANCES

The goal – for Z to receive the friendship
of Y, who's on X without anyone moving
from their posture or stance. Repeat, rehearse
several times on carpet, and then upon
a platform or dais. Top mounts must always
have around their bulk a bond suspended
from the spectrum of appropriate response.
Daring each other and gaining access
to some vitally transmissible truth,
X charms Y, who rezones an anxious path
into a matter of knowing – sudden, global.
Y draws a radiantly heightened mode
and enchants perception, then braids threads
and arranges souls in X's intimacy.
Z warned away from what must remain
nameless. Y obliging by finding purchase
on X's whole world forever. Y subsists,
climbs out of ontological impoverishment
to a private, inchoate cluster, coming
to a free, plural pose. Next, X beckons Z
out of some desert-like state. From there,
Z carries energies into new channels.
All stand suasive. Freeze inveterate. Then veer
forward to glory to longing is not a static thing.

EXTRACTS FROM LETTERS OF SUPPORT

Denver, Colo.

JTG, hailing from Roanoke, Virginia, has provided us with an apparatus of such *savoir faire*. A gift! Such minute instructions! And those illustrations! You ought not to charge less than twenty dollars. I do not know for sure, but I think you could get more. I shall be very glad to purchase eleven copies for my whole family as soon as it is published. Please let me know. Tumble, tumble.

London, England

I believe in tumbling. It makes a person quick, agile, and very sure-footed. A form of sport popular when properly taught. We have no good book on the subject; we need a couple. For those interested, try TFA, written by one who has much experience in actual somersaults, who understands the mechanisms of musculature: Gwathmey, of Nashville, Tennessee. Just the person to compile such a modus operandi. A clever performer, a convivial teacher, an educated physician. I have looked over the MS. I endorse it.

Montreal, Canada

I am glad to find someone able to draw the veil from a sphere of agility which the professional acrobat has so long kept shrouded in mystery. The reducing of various feats of gymnastics to a progressive sequence is a difficult task indeed, but this kinetoscope method will make clear what would otherwise require pages of description. Your oeuvre assists anyone of ordinary ability to master the rudiments of this performative art. Also appeals to a much wider scope of all who admire nimbleness. Also also gives some idea of the difficulties mastered by the expert, whose breathtaking efforts we will more fully appreciate.

Let me tell you, the combinations of bucking broncos are infinite. The inventive coach can repeat the same exercises in a different order, making new moves out of old ones, and thus keeping up the interest and enthusiasm from day to day. Select ten or twelve from Gwathmey's list and give as a drill. Change the sequence and repeat for next lesson, and then give a completely different workout on the third day to keep things exciting. Then return to BB on the fourth day, etc. As you advance, you can devise, make up, and hatch your own combos. Huzzah!

Mexico City, Mexico
Your guide, just announced, will be hailed with glee by thousands of young people who seek this brand of stunt work. The photographs that illuminate your pages provide intrinsic value to bumblers who have no talented teacher to explain each step. If the element of risk grows greater than the need for physicality, as some claim, then your softback, giving such graphic pictures of bodies passing through different stages of change, cannot fail to reduce that danger to a degree in which every budding gymnast will find comfort. I therefore recommend your timely little number to all who may wish to revel in the delightful pastime, present time, tumble-time.

Richmond, Virg.
True, we neglected our duties and studies. True, we displayed an air of careless indifference. True, we frequented a billiards saloon without permission. True, we threw a brick through a professor's dorm window, leading to our dismissal from VMI. So what? We toured with a circus troupe. We taught in the YMCAs of Des Moines and Omaha. We established the Summer School for High Culture at Vandy U. Other resumé highlights include: co-presidents of the Bicycle Club, heads of the Gymnastic Society, faculty advisors to the Chi Chapter of Kappa Alpha, this magnum opus and its hearty reception by physical directors the world over (and others who are interested). Take that!

Chicago, Ill.

I have to say, for some actions, you may find the removal of clothes is actually beneficial, and for others, it is an absolute necessity. Clothes impede grip, and the lack of purchase quite often interferes with the success of certain exercises.

Paris, France

It has always seemed to me that the constructivist approach to teaching is the most useful, and I know this discipline in your knowledgeable care will help enormously in instructing a difficult branch of somatic rendering. Imagine student-led, consensual, inquiry-based learning. Now double it. Triple it. Quick question: don't we all exist in a constant state of partial contraction? Why yes, we do. Enough said. Accept no substitute. Quality guaranteed.

Boston, Mass.

In physical education, as in mental and spiritual enlightenment, there endure some complex fields adapted to the few and not the many. Acrobatics is one of these. Controlled, cultivated, undertaken by trained bodies. A pleasure to know that a manual on this specialty will soon tumble into our laps, prepared and furnished for our perusal by one so capable to issue forth as Gwathmey, of Vanderbilt University. We wait, impatiently, to sniff its leaves of grass.

New York, N.Y.

For sound people, tumbling is one of the best and most exhilarating exercises when refined under suitable conditions. Of course, toppling over on a brick sidewalk differs from cascading on a hair-stuffed mattress. Can one learn to fall head over heels after reaching maturity? Certainly, as many first-class tumblers did not commence until after their second child. At the age of thirty-three, convinced to take the plunge under Gwathmey, and, with the aid of his technique, I succeeded in learning to do over fifty different moves and combinations and impress everyone, my wife included.

Kansas City, Mo.

Two words: jock strap. Gwathmey's reference text is the 'Mike Murphy' jockey supporter of the Spalding Athletic Library. AKA the best!

Toronto, Canada

I approve of your idea of getting out such a volume, though I would take out the more advanced manoeuvres. Or, if you keep them in, mark all with an asterisk (*), so that amateurs will not try these. In subsequent editions, do think of adding the pommel horse, rings, the vault, bars, the balance beam. That being said, I celebrate this achievement. No other kind of human symphony exists that will so tunefully develop every part of your euphony and so provide new harmonies to the music of tumbledown.

Madrid, Spain

I believe that the greater the command a person has over their body, and tumbling undoubtedly increases this fluency, the better off they are. I wish you all the success that life has to offer.

These poems are derived from, and all the illustrations come from:

TUMBLING FOR AMATEURS
By
JAMES T. GWATHMEY, M.D.

As well as:

GROUND TUMBLING
By
HENRY WALTER WORTH

Both published by:

AMERICAN SPORTS PUBLISHING COMPANY
21 Warren Street, New York
Copyright 1910
By
American Sports Publishing Company
New York

NOTES AND ACKNOWLEDGEMENTS

Tumbling For Amateurs is a modern reimagining of an old sporting manual written by a distant relative. The original text literally fell into my lap, and I was immediately taken by the descriptions of various feats of tumbling as well as accompanying illustrations and associated metaphors. I tried to peel back these layers to find the possibility of a hidden subculture of desire, both homosocial and homoerotic. This collection aims to give voice to a suppressed existence of the early twentieth century. James Tayloe Gwathmey's original text of the same name was published in 1910 as part of Spalding's Athletic Library and was gifted to me by someone who recognized the last name and thought that it must be poetry. JTG really is my distant relative: my second cousin, four times removed. I wanted to write the book that my friend thought *Tumbling for Amateurs* was.

Thank you to the New Brunswick Arts Board and the Canada Council for the Arts for their support during the writing of these poems. Thank you to the first readers: Lily Smallwood, Phoebe Wang, and thom vernon. Thanks to everyone at Coach House Books: Alana Wilcox, Crystal Sikma, and James Lindsay. Thanks especially especially to Nasser Hussain. Tumble tumble.

James Tayloe Gwathmey, centre in the white shirt,
was coach of the Vanderbilt Gymnasium Team in 1899,
the year he graduated from the Vanderbilt School of Medicine.

Matthew Gwathmey was born in Richmond, Virginia, and currently lives in Fredericton, New Brunswick, on Wolastoqey Territory, with his partner Lily and their five children. He studied creative writing at the University of Virginia and recently completed his PhD at the University of New Brunswick. He has work published in the *Malahat Review, Crazyhorse, Prairie Fire,* the *Fiddlehead,* and the *Iowa Review,* as well as other literary magazines. His first poetry collection, *Our Latest in Folktales,* was published by Brick Books in the spring of 2019.

Typeset in Arno and Futura.

Printed at the Coach House on bpNichol Lane in Toronto, Ontario, on Zephyr Antique Laid paper, which was manufactured, acid-free, in Saint-Jérôme, Quebec, from second-growth forests. This book was printed with vegetable-based ink on a 1973 Heidelberg KORD offset litho press. Its pages were folded on a Baumfolder, gathered by hand, bound on a Sulby Auto-Minabinda, and trimmed on a Polar single-knife cutter.

Coach House is on the traditional territory of many nations, including the Mississaugas of the Credit, the Anishnabeg, the Chippewa, the Haudenosaunee, and the Wendat peoples, and is now home to many diverse First Nations, Inuit, and Métis peoples. We acknowledge that Toronto is covered by Treaty 13 with the Mississaugas of the Credit. We are grateful to live and work on this land.

Edited by Nasser Hussain
Cover and interior design by Crystal Sikma
Author photo by Chantal R. Mercier

Coach House Books
80 bpNichol Lane
Toronto ON M5S 3J4
Canada

416 979 2217
800 367 6360

mail@chbooks.com
www.chbooks.com